DISCOVER&
LEARN

HEALTHY EATING

by

Gemma McMullen

©2017
Book Life
King's Lynn
Norfolk PE30 4LS

ISBN: 978-1-78637-072-3

Written by:
Gemma McMullen

Edited by:
Grace Jones

Designed by:
Drue Rintoul

CONTENTS

Words in **bold** are explained in the glossary on page 31.

Page 4   The Food Groups

Page 8   Meat and Fish

Page 12   Carbohydrates

Page 16   Milk and Dairy Products

Page 20   Fats and Sugars

Page 24   Fruit and Vegetables

Page 30   What About Drinks?

Page 31   Glossary

Page 32   Index

THE
FOOD GROUPS

WHAT ARE FOOD GROUPS?

A food group is a collection of foods that share similar **nutritional properties**. There are five main food groups: meats and fish (proteins), carbohydrates, milk and dairy products, fats and sugars and fruit and vegetables. It is important that we eat enough foods from each of these food groups in order to achieve a balanced diet.

WHAT IS A BALANCED DIET?

A balanced diet is one which includes regular intake of enough food from each of the food groups. The recommended portion of each food group varies (see diagram opposite). Eating a balanced diet will ensure that your body receives all the nutrients that it needs to stay healthy.

A BALANCED PLATE

This pie chart shows how much of each food group is needed to maintain a healthy diet.

CARBOHYDRATES

FRUITS AND VEGETABLES

MEAT AND FISH

FATS AND SUGARS

MILK AND DAIRY PRODUCTS

WHY EAT A BALANCED DIET?

Food and drink is the fuel that our bodies use; we need food and drink to give us energy to breathe, move and grow.
There are so many different foods out there, that we are given a choice daily about what we eat or don't eat. Our bodies can only be as healthy as the food that we give them.
It is important that we eat a variety of foods, so that our bodies can get all of the nutrients that they need. We should try to balance our diets, so that the portions that we eat are similar to the pie chart on page 5.

WHAT ARE CALORIES?

Calories are the units which the energy of food is measured in. Different foods are assigned a calorie content, depending on the ingredients within them. We should each eat a certain amount of calories each day. The recommended amount depends on our age, size and whether we are male or female.

OVERWEIGHT OR UNDERWEIGHT

We all have different body types and no two human bodies are the same. It is important that we maintain a healthy weight for our own body type. Eating too much food can result in a person being overweight. Equally, eating too little food can result in the opposite. A body cannot work completely effectively if it is overweight or underweight.

MEAT
AND FISH

Meat and fish are foods we eat that come from animals. Meat and fish can be eaten as an important part of our diets. They contain proteins, which our bodies need. Protein is good for our bodies because it helps the body to grow and to repair itself.

OTHER SOURCES OF PROTEIN

As well as eating the meat of animals, we also eat animal products, such as eggs. Eggs, beans and nuts are all good sources of protein. Protein helps our bodies to stay healthy. Our muscles and organs are mainly made of protein.

WHICH MEATS DO WE EAT?

Meat includes lamb from young sheep, beef from cows, pork from pigs and poultry from birds such as chickens or turkeys. Depending on the place that someone lives, other animals may also be used as meat sources. A butcher prepares the meat so that we can buy different cuts, depending on how we plan to use the meat. For example, different parts of a pig are used to make sausages, bacon and pork chops. The better quality the meat is, the more expensive it will be. Pork meat can come from several places on a pig.

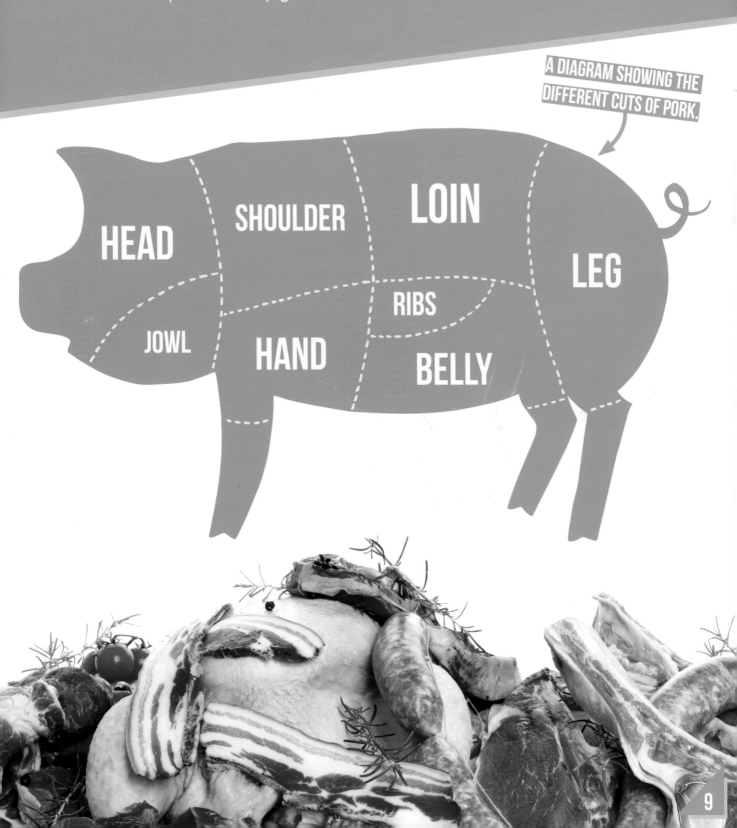

A DIAGRAM SHOWING THE DIFFERENT CUTS OF PORK.

HEAD

SHOULDER

LOIN

LEG

RIBS

JOWL

HAND

BELLY

HEALTHY PROTEINS

To have a balanced diet, we all need some protein. Some sources of protein are better for our bodies than others. White meat and fish have a much lower fat content than red meat. It is better to eat white meat and fish more frequently than red meat.

UNHEALTHY PROTEINS

As with all foods, the way that we cook meat can affect how healthy it is. Food that is fried is not as good for us as food that is grilled. The amount of fat in a cut of meat can make it less healthy too, as can the addition of other food stuffs such as salt.

FRIED BACON HAS A HIGH FAT CONTENT AND CONTAINS A LOT OF SALT.

PROCESSED MEAT

Processed meats are meats which are not in their natural state. Usually other things have been added to them. Processed foods are generally not very good for us, so they should be eaten in small quantities. Ready meals, such as lasagne, chicken casserole or fish pie, often include processed meat or fish. It is always better to cook your own foods from scratch where possible.

VEGETARIANISM

Some people choose not to eat meat at all. They are called vegetarians. People who decide not to eat any animal products are called vegans. Vegetarians and vegans must make sure that they still have plenty of protein in their diets by substituting meat with other protein rich food sources.

BEANS, LENTILS AND PULSES ARE SOURCES OF HEALTHY PROTEINS FOR VEGETARIANS.

CARBOHYDRATES

Bread, pasta, potatoes and foods made from grains are all high in carbohydrates. Eating carbohydrates is good for our bodies because it gives us energy. It is important that we eat enough carbohydrates, but eating too many can result in a person becoming overweight.

TOO MUCH OF A GOOD THING

The human body converts carbohydrates into energy, so that we can breathe, move and do exercise. If we do not use up all of the energy that is put into our bodies, the energy stays in our bodies and is stored as fat. If this process is repeated often, then a person will start to put on too much weight.

WHICH CARBOHYDRATES DO WE EAT?

Grains are small, hard, dry seeds from plants. Oats, wheat and rice are all grains. Foods containing large amounts of grain are high in carbohydrates. Rice is usually cooked or used to make rice products, such as rice cakes or rice milk. Breakfast cereals are made using grains such as oats and corn.

FLOUR

Some grains are ground down into flour. Flour is used to make bread and pasta, which are both foods high in carbohydrates. Bread comes in many forms and can be savoury or sweet. Pasta is used in savoury dishes, such as lasagne and spaghetti bolognese.

HEALTHY CARBOHYDRATES

Foods high in carbohydrates contain starch, which our bodies need. The right amount of carbohydrates should be eaten as part of every meal. Healthier foods are the foods that have been made using the whole of the grain rather than only part of the grain.

BROWN BREAD IS HEALTHIER THAN WHITE BECAUSE IT IS MADE USING WHOLE GRAINS, RATHER THAN ONLY PART LIKE WHITE BREAD.

UNHEALTHY CARBOHYDRATES

Some carbohydrates are less healthy because other foods such as sugar and fat have been added to them. Pizza makes a delicious treat but can be high in fat and have a high calorie content. Cakes, doughnuts and biscuits are high in sugar and fat and should not be eaten too often.

POTATOES

The potato is a vegetable but is classed as a starchy food. The way that potatoes are cooked determines how healthy they are. Jacket potatoes are healthy because they are baked and still have their skin (the healthiest parts). Be careful with toppings though, as they can be high in fat.

CHIPS CONTAIN A LOT OF OIL AND FAT.

BREAKFAST CEREALS

Many of us eat breakfast cereals as a healthy start to the day. Breakfast is a good time to eat a meal high in carbohydrates because a person has the whole day to burn off their energy. Some cereals, however, have a very high sugar content, so choose your breakfast carefully.

MILK AND
DAIRY PRODUCTS

Milk is a white liquid produced by mammals to feed their young. It contains high levels of protein, fat and calcium, all of which our bodies need to develop and grow. Most of the milk that we drink comes from cows, but the milk from many mammals is safe for human **consumption**. Milk can be drunk on its own or used as part of another drink. Milk is often used on cereals, and can be used to make other food products. Dairy products are products which have been made using milk. These include cheese and yoghurt.

WHICH DAIRY PRODUCTS DO WE EAT?

Cheese is a dairy product. It is produced in special factories and can take quite a long time to make. There are hundreds of different types of cheese. Cheese can be eaten alone or used as an ingredient for other meals.

Yoghurt is a dairy product. Natural yoghurt has a sour taste, so yoghurt is often sweetened before it is sold.

Butter is a dairy product that is made using only the fat content of milk. It can be used as a spread or as a baking ingredient.

HEALTHY DAIRY

Milk and dairy products contain protein, which helps our bodies to grow and to repair themselves. They also contain fat, which is good for our bodies in **moderation**. Milk products are a very good source of calcium, which is a mineral that helps to keep our teeth and bones strong.

UNHEALTHY DAIRY

Dairy products include more ingredients than milk alone. The addition of foods such as sugars can make the products unhealthy. Milkshakes, ice cream and sweetened yoghurts should not be eaten too often.

FARMING MILK

Selling milk is a big business. Dairy farmers keep dairy cows especially for their milk. The cows can be milked by hand, but on large farms special machines extract the milk. The milk is then prepared by different machines before being bottled for use.

MILK FROM OTHER ANIMALS

Whilst most milk in the UK comes from cows, it is perfectly safe to drink the milk of goats or sheep also. In other parts of the world, different **native** animals are used for milk. Water buffaloes are the main source of milk in South Asia and reindeer milk is popular in northern regions of the world.

REINDEER

SHEEP

WATER BUFFALO

19

FATS AND SUGARS

Our bodies need a small amount of fat to maintain a healthy diet. One source of fat that we can eat is animal fat. Sometimes the animal fat in our food is visible, but it is also found in many foods which we may not expect. For this reason, vegetarians and vegans must be careful when choosing their food.

VISIBLE FAT

ANIMAL FAT CAN BE USED IN ALL OF THESE PRODUCTS.

Oils are fats that can be **obtained** from plants. Cooking oils such as sunflower oil, olive oil and vegetable oil come from plants. We use these oils to fry our foods in. Sometimes oil is poured onto salad or used as a dip for bread.

COOKING OIL

SUGAR

Sugar is a sweet substance which comes from plants. Some foods, such as fruits, are high in natural sugars. Other foods have sugar added to them. This sugar is grown from plants such as sugar cane or sugar beet and is treated to remove any **impurities**. We call this sugar refined sugar. It is added to foods to make them taste sweeter.

Some sugars are more visible than others. We know that there is sugar in sweets and fizzy drinks, but even savoury foods like soups can contain refined sugar. Flavoured yoghurt, pasta sauce and even dried fruits have sugar added to them.

SUGAR CANE

DRIED FRUIT

YOGHURT

HEALTHY FATS

It is a **misconception** that all fat is bad for us. We need fats in our diet to keep us healthy. Fats give us energy and keep our skin and organs healthy. The healthiest fats are the natural fats that occur in fish, nuts, fruits and vegetables.

AVOCADO

NUTS

SALMON

UNHEALTHY FATS

Too much fat in our diets, however, can make us overweight. Saturated fat is a type of fat that is not good for our bodies. High levels of it can be found in a lot of processed foods, such as cakes, pastries, pizza and pork pies.

CHOCOLATE CAKE AND PIZZA BOTH CONTAIN UNHEALTHY FATS.

HEALTHY SUGARS

Some sugar in our diets is good because sugar is a carbohydrate which gives us energy. As with fats, the healthiest sugars are those which occur naturally in food. Sugars in fruits and vegetables are better than added refined sugars.

UNHEALTHY SUGARS

We need to be careful with refined sugars which are added to foods. Eating too much sugar will result in weight gain. Another big problem for those who eat too much of any sugar is that it is bad for our teeth.

FRUIT AND
VEGETABLES

Looking back at the recommended portion plate on page 5, you will notice that the proportion of fruit and vegetables that should be eaten is one of the largest of any food group. You may have also heard of governments advising people to eat a certain number of portions of fruit and vegetables every day.

WHY ARE FRUIT AND VEGETABLES SO GOOD?

Fruit and vegetables contain important nutrients that our bodies need. These include vitamins and minerals that help to keep us healthy. Fruit and vegetables also have low fat content and contain only natural sugars.

FRUIT OR VEGETABLE?

'Fruit' is a **botanical** term, it describes the part of a flowering plant that holds the seeds. 'Vegetable' is a **culinary** term, and many of the vegetables that we eat are in fact the fruits of the plant. Courgettes, for example, have seeds inside them, which actually makes them a fruit. Other vegetables that we eat are parts of plants. When we eat leeks, we are eating the stem of a plant. When we eat cabbage, we are eating the leaves of a plant. We tend to think of sweet-tasting plant parts as fruit, and savoury tasting plant parts as vegetables.

COURGETTE (FRUIT)

CABBAGE (VEGETABLE)

LEEK (VEGETABLE)

WHICH FRUITS DO WE EAT?

The list of fruits that we eat is **extensive**, and depends somewhat on the country in which we live. The **climate** of a place will determine which fruits grow there. That said, modern **exportation** of food means that we are easily able to obtain fruits from other continents.

HOW DO WE EAT FRUIT?

Fruit is **versatile** because it can be eaten raw or cooked. We can eat the flesh of the fruit, which can be soft or hard. Some fruit skins are edible, whilst others we peel away. Many fruits can be pressed to make fruit juices.

WHICH VEGETABLES DO WE EAT?

As with fruit, the vegetables that we eat can be determined by where we live. Different plants need different weather in order to grow. For this reason, vegetables are also **seasonal**. The more variety we can eat, the better it is for our diet.

HOW DO WE EAT VEGETABLES?

Vegetables can be eaten raw or cooked, though we tend to cook them out of preference. Raw vegetables are actually better for us, because cooking removes some of their nutrients. For this reason, it is better not to over cook vegetables. Vegetables can be eaten alone, or mixed with other ingredients to make delicious meals.

BROCCOLI

HEALTHY FRUIT AND VEGETABLES

Fruit and vegetables are very good for us. The properties in them help to keep our organs healthy and help us to fight diseases, such as heart disease. Research suggests that they may even help to prevent cancer. Fruit and vegetables should be eaten every day and as part of every meal. They generally have a low calorie content, so you can eat plenty as part of your daily allowance. They also contain lots of fibre, which is needed to keep your digestive system in good shape.

UNHEALTHY FRUIT AND VEGETABLES

The only reason that fruit and vegetables may be considered unhealthy, is the way in which they are prepared. The apples in apple pies, for example, are mixed with sugar and pastry, making them more of a treat food than an everyday one. There is a large amount of sugar in foods such as jam too, and in fruit juice. Whilst natural sugar is better for us than refined sugar, it can still cause problems for our teeth, if eaten in too large a quantity.

JAM AND APPLE PIES BOTH CONTAIN A LOT OF SUGAR.

SOME FOOD PACKAGING CAN BE DECEIVING, AS IT TELLS YOU THE AMOUNT OF NUTRITIONAL FRUIT IN ITS GOODS, BUT NOT THE AMOUNT OF ADDED SUGAR.

WHAT ABOUT DRINKS?

Drinks play an important role in our diets. It is important that we drink enough liquid every day. Drinks keep our bodies **hydrated**. The more energy that we expend throughout the day, the more liquid that our bodies need. As with foods, some drinks are healthier than others, and drinks do need to be counted as part of our calorie allowance.

WHICH DRINKS ARE BEST?

As with food, the more natural a product is, the better it is for our bodies. Water is the base of any liquid, and is most healthy in its natural form. Milk is also good for us. Other drinks, however, often have a lot of additives, so we need to be careful. Milkshakes and energy drinks should only be drunk occasionally.

GLOSSARY

31

botanical	scientific, relating to plants
climate	the weather in a certain area
consumption	use
culinary	for cooking
exportation	moving goods out of a country
extensive	affecting a large area
hydrated	to have enough water
impurities	impure parts
misconception	misunderstanding
moderation	avoiding large amounts or excess
native	belonging to a place of birth
nutritional properties	values given to parts of foods or drinks
obtained	got from
seasonal	relating to a particular season
versatile	able to be used in many ways

31

INDEX

calories 7, 14, 28, 30

carbohydrates 4–5, 12–15, 23

dairy 4–5, 16–19

energy 6–7, 12, 15, 22–23, 30

fats 4–5, 10, 12, 14–18, 20-24

fish 4–5, 8–11, 22

food groups 4–5, 24

fruits 4–5, 21–29

meats 4–5, 8–11

milk 4–5, 16–19, 30

minerals 18, 24

nutrition 4, 29

proteins 4, 8, 10–11, 16, 18

sugars 4–5, 14–15, 18, 20, 23–24, 29

vegetables 4–5, 15, 20, 22–24, 29

vegetarians 11, 20

vitamins 24